Also by Nick Butterworth and Mick Inkpen:

The House on the Rock, The Lost Sheep,
The Two Sons, The Precious Pearl,
The Magpie's Story, The Mouse's Story,
The Fox's Story, The Cat's Story.

Copyright © 1989 Nick Butterworth & Mick Inkpen
First published in 1989 by Marshall Pickering.
Marshall Pickering is an imprint of Collins Religious Division,
part of the Collins Publishing Group, 8 Grafton Street, London W1X 3LA.

Reprinted 1990

British Library CIP Data
Butterworth, Nick
  The good Samaritan
  1. Bible. N.T. Parables: Good Samaritan
  I. Title   II. Inkpen, Mick   III. Series
  226'.8

  ISBN 0-551-01670-1

Printed and bound in Italy

The Good Stranger

Nick Butterworth and Mick Inkpen

Marshall Pickering

Here is a man. He is going on a long journey.

He packs some sandwiches and a flask of tea. Then he climbs onto his donkey.

'Giddyup!'

Soon he has left the town behind him.

The sun is hot and the long climb up into the hills makes his donkey puff.

The path winds between high rocks. It is a dark place, full of shadows.

'I don't like it here,' says the man. He has a funny feeling that someone is watching him.

Suddenly there is a shout!
Robbers! Three of them!

They steal his donkey and
all his belongings. And they
whack him on the head
with his own stick!

Poor man. He is left lying on the path. His head is bleeding and he cannot move his legs.

He lies here for a long time, then, finally he falls asleep.

After a while, someone comes
along the path. He is wearing
fine clothes. A bishop.

He stops, then hurries past,
pretending not to see. Perhaps
he is late for important business.

Perhaps he is afraid.

The man wakes up and starts
to call for help.

Ah! Here comes someone.
A man in a wig. A judge.

'Help! Help!'

But the judge pretends not
to hear and he hurries past.
Just like the bishop.

The sun rises high in the sky. The man is hot. His throat is dry. But here come more footsteps! Who is it?

Oh no! It is a stranger from a foreign country. He has no friends here. Why should he stop to help?

But the stranger does stop.
He speaks kindly to the man in
foreign words, and helps him
to drink some water.

He washes his wounds and
carefully puts a bandage round
his head.

The stranger helps the man up onto his donkey. He puts his arm around him to stop him falling off, and gently leads him down the path.

At the next town the stranger
finds an inn. He puts the man
to bed and pays the innkeeper.

'Look after him,' he says,
until I get back.'

Jesus says, 'Which one was like a good neighbour?
The bishop, the judge or the stranger?